Britain's Buses
in the seventies

Edited by E. L. Cornwell
and John Parke

First published 1976

ISBN 0 7110 0741 1

PUBLISHED BY
IAN ALLAN LTD
TERMINAL HOUSE·SHEPPERTON·TW17 8AS·ENGLAND
TELEPHONE: WALTON ON THAMES 28950

Covers: Front: One of the Leyland Atlantean AN68/1s with 78-seat East Lancs bodies delivered to City of Nottingham Transport in 1975 *(T. W. Moore);*
Back cover above: Many of the Albion Lowlanders of the SBG have been transferred to the Highland Omnibuses fleet including this one from Western SMT seen on one of the Inverness local services *(Gavin Booth);*
Back cover below: a Crosville Bristol LH negotiates a hairpin bend on its way to Aberystwyth in countryside very typical of this area. *(A. Moyes)*

Printed in the United Kingdom by Crampton & Sons Ltd, Sawston, Cambridge.

PRESENTATION of a selection of pictures of buses and coaches at work in Great Britain in the nineteen-seventies must tend inevitably to underline the trend that there has been towards the preponderance of underfloor- and rear-engined vehicles. It is true that they had been common in the previous decade but the institution of the bus grant scheme and the strong desire of stage service providers to change over to one-man operation as a partial palliative to increasing labour costs combined to hasten the process. It follows that more and more vehicles tend to look somewhat similar and the policy of the National Bus Company in standardising the livery of its subsidiaries has taken that process also a stage further. The decision to adopt a white livery for express coaches was greeted with some displeasure by the traditionalists but the change became generally accepted as time passed and it is of some interest that white has now been adopted by a considerable number of independent operators.

The decline in the number of passengers has provoked the withdrawal of some bus services and a change in operator of others, with the smaller concerns filling gaps left by the larger. The practice has depended a good deal upon the attitude of the local authority involved, with some councils far more ready than others to support essential facilities. A newcomer to bus operation has been the Post Office and Scotland in particular has benefited from its versatility as have some rural areas in England—one or two typical operating scenes are included.

There are also views of rural and urban workings in a variety of surroundings with emphasis where possible of the active life that a public service vehicle leads. The consolidation during the seventies of the passenger transport executives and, indeed, the creation of new ones has meant that they have tended to claim particular attention and there have been many well-justified candidates for which there was insufficient space.

All-in-all, however, the collection should afford a general impression of the appearance of the British bus industry in the first half of the current decade.

Yates
LEOPARD
LMA 60P

80 FEARNHEAD
Crosville
LEYLAND NATIONAL
RFM 877M

Above left: Typifying the medium-sized independent coach operator, a 1975 Plaxton-bodied Leyland Leopard of Yates Tours, Runcorn, is seen at Gretna Green returning from the Edinburgh Tattoo. *G. Coxon*

Above: Alexander bodywork was mounted on a batch of Daimler Fleetlines delivered to Yorkshire Woollen District in 1971. No 29 is seen conveying a special party.

Left: A Leyland National of Crosville in Arpley Station yard, Warrington, on a local route operated prior to April 1974 by Lancashire United. *A. Moyes*

Left: In the summer of 1971 a party of enthusiasts hired an Aldershot & District Dennis Loline III with Weymann bodywork for a tour of Scotland. It is seen on the Tay road bridge. *P. Gascoine*

Below: The morning mail for Lochgoilhead and Carrick Castle is transferred from Western SMT ML2180, a Leyland Leopard on the Glasgow-Tarbert service, to ex-MacBrayne Bedford ME3 at the top of Rest and Be Thankful at a time when the connecting service was still maintained by Western SMT. *Iain MacGregor*

Right: The first all-over advertising bus of an independent operator was this Guy Arab IV of AA Motor Services, Ayr, originally in the East Kent fleet and intermediately with Graham of Paisley. *Gavin Booth*

Below: Although the arrangements between the Scottish Bus Group and the National Bus Company for the exchange of Bristol VRTs for Lodekkas were by then well under way, this VRT was still on a Kilmarnock town service of Western SMT in June 1973. *Gavin Booth*

Left: Previously with Venture Transport (Newcastle) this Duple-bodied Bedford SB5 of Saltburn Motor Services is climbing the hairpin bend above Saltburn Pier soon after the takeover of the company by Cleveland Transit.
M. Fowler

Below: An AEC Reliance with Plaxton Derwent II bodywork in Dewsbury on the service thence to Mirfield operated by J. J. Longstaff & Sons Ltd of the latter town.
M. Fowler

Right: Specially bought for services from its Altrincham depot traversing very low bridges and narrow roads, North Western Road Car replaced low-roofed Bedford VALs with ECW-bodied Bristol REs of this type in 1971. *R. L. Wilson*

Bottom right: In NBC poppy red, a Northern General Routemaster enters Durham in the summer of 1974. *M. Fowler*

4U HALEBARNS
MONDAY JUNE 28
AGATHA CHRISTIE'S
FIDDLERS
Whisky galore!
NORTH WESTERN
SJA 373J
STU 615J

CROOK
Littlewoods

Left: An increasingly common sight in Scotland represented by a Commer postbus in Elvie (Fife) on a Leven-based route introduced in 1975 and serving New Gilston.
Edward Shirras

Below: Typical Hebridean scenery with two Plaxton-bodied Bedfords of Morrison of Northton returning from Stornoway to Tarbert along the main road to connect with an evening ferry service to Uig (Skye). The operation passed to Highland and later to Harris Garage.
D. J. Currie

Right, top to bottom:
One of 16 Willowbrook-bodied Ford R1014s delivered to Highland Omnibuses in 1973. Operations in the Outer Hebrides have since been relinquished. *Ford Motor Co*

The Westerbus operations of M. Taylor, Badcaul, have in some cases substituted for former Highland Omnibuses facilities and in others developed new routes. A Ford Transit with Moseley Envoy bodywork stands at Dingwall Station on the service to Aultbea in 1973. *Alan Millar*

A 1973 addition to the fleet of Sutherland Transport which operates long routes into the sparsely-populated country north-west of Lairg was this Bedford VAS 16-seater with mail and freight compartments in its Willowbrook body. *C. B. Golding*

NORTHERN Tynesider
SHOP AT Binns
NORTH SHIELDS
3000
MCN 30K

Left: Originally a conventional Leyland Titan PD3/4 in the associated Tyneside fleet, the Northern Group modified the bus in order to determine the practicability of converting its Routemasters for convenient one-man operation.
Duncan Bulmer

Right: To mark one Christmas Bradford adorned three buses in a special seasonable livery. One of them was 320, an Alexander-bodied Daimler Fleetline. *John Fozard*

Below: One of the earlier Leyland Atlanteans to enter the Sheffield Transport fleet was 885, one of a batch with Metro-Cammell bodywork here seen at The Moor.
Terry Whitham

ADSWOOD WEMBLEY HOTEL
24
SOUTHERN
5080
NDB 353

Left: Crossley bodywork was fitted to this Leyland Tiger Cub, one of four which passed to SELNEC with the Stockport undertaking.
C. B. Marsh

Above right: A Bedford J2 with Duple bodywork inherited from the Wallasey undertaking by the Merseyside PTE in Liscard on the shoppers service instituted by Wallasey. *R. L. Wilson*

Right: More common in Scotland than in England, the Albion Lowlanders have tended over the years to gravitate to the Highland Omnibuses fleet, as was the case with Highland's AL41 originally in the fleet of Western SMT.
Alan Millar

Below: Rebuilding of the notorious Dunham Massey canal bridge on the Altrincham-Dunham-Warrington service of Crosville (ex-North Western) caused diversion in 1973 over a 4-ton-limit canal bridge and the transfer to Warrington of five Bristol SC4LKs, one being SSG642.
A. Moyes

26 TALBOT SQUARE
VIA
MARTON
571
OFR 971M
PRIZE

HASLINGDEN
ROSSENDALE
ETC 660J

Left: Two of the then new AEC Swifts with 47-seat Marshall bodies in service with Blackpool Corporation at South Pier in the spring of 1974. *Gavin Booth*

Below left: East Lancashire-bodied, this Leyland Leopard of Rossendale Transport is seen in Rawtenstall in June 1971. *M. A. Penn*

Above right: Originally in the Birkenhead fleet, a Leyland Atlantean of Merseyside PTE with Northern Counties body in Liverpool bound for a Wallasey destination. *R. L. Wilson*

Right: Ordered by North Western Road Car, this Bristol VRT with Eastern Coach Works body was delivered to SELNEC Cheshire but had the Cheshire flash painted out. It is in Mersey Square Stockport. *A. Moyes*

Below: Independent operators in the Doncaster area of South Yorkshire tend to buy their vehicles new, as H. Wilson Ltd, operating as Premier, did this Alexander-bodied Leyland Atlantean. *M. Fowler*

National
Westminster
Bank
4
Piccadilly
Station
1723
2p Fare No Change
XVU 353M

Left: Greater Manchester PTE operates an intensive city centre service with Seddon midibuses, one of which is seen in King Street, a previously unserved thoroughfare. *A. Moyes*

Right: This Leyland Leopard of Venture Transport (Newcastle) wears the livery of yellow with a maroon strip and cream roof, which has become more or less a matter of memory. *G. Coxon*

Below: By the time this rear-engined Foden was photographed in Brechin, Angus, in the autumn of 1970 the type, which was never plentiful, was rarely to be seen on the road. *M. J. Fenton*

LIVERPOOL RD
AUGHTON RD
16
106
GFY 406
BUS STOP TO TOWN

Facing page: An all-Leyland Titan PD2/3 of Southport Corporation with the Farington-type body. *M. A. Taylor*

Left: Standing in Dundee bus station in Alexander (Northern) livery in June 1971, this Leyland Titan PD2/20 of 1957 with Northern Counties body had recently been transferred from Western SMT. *Edward Shirras*

Below: By the time this Roe-bodied AEC Regent V of 1963 was photographed at Gipton in November 1974 there were few rear-entrance double-deckers remaining in service in Leeds. *C. J. Spring*

Above: In Bishop Auckland and bound for Newcastle, where it began its life with the municipal undertaking (later Tyneside PTE No199), is this 1961 Alexander-bodied Leyland Atlantean of OK Motor Services. *G. R. Mills*

Below: Park Royal bodywork was mounted on this Leyland Atlantean AN68/1, among the last to be delivered to Sunderland District in NBC blue livery before the Northern Group began to assimilate its associated fleet. It too is in Bishop Auckland. *V. H. Darling*

Above: In the red and cream of the St Helens division of Merseyside PTE is a former Birkenhead Leyland Titan PD2/40. *R. L. Wilson*

Above right: Originally Wigan No4 and then Greater Manchester 3333 this Leyland Atlantean AN68/2 was one of only 10 rear-engined vehicles taken over. *T. E. Sutch*

Right: In Bolton bus station soon after delivery in 1971, a Marshall-bodied Bristol RE of Ribble Motor Services. *G. H. F. Atkins*

Below: Halifax Leyland Leopard No 239 leaving Lumbutts en route from Mankinholes to Todmorden in the week preceding the actual merger of the Halifax and Todmorden undertakings on August 2 1971. *A. Moyes*

TO LET
SPORTS & T
6A
Aldwych Fleet St
Bank Liverpool St
Shoreditch Hackney
WATERLOO
THE KARATE KILLERS
RITZ
THE KARATE KILLERS
RITZ
FRAMES' TOURS LD
MRO 144 D
JJD 549 D
TORIA
BLT 842

Left: Typifying a Central London scene of the 1970s, this view of Queen Victoria Street shows a London Transport RML preceding a senior and shorter RM version. *London Transport*

Above: Many of the major operators in holiday and tourist areas can justify the use of open-top buses. A Southern Vectis Bristol Lodekka converted in the early 1970s approaches Sandown. *T. W. Moore*

Right: Among early users of all-over advertising on buses was Barclaycard and the introduction of its 1972 campaign was marked by the display in St Paul's Churchyard, London, of, from the left, a Park Royal-bodied Daimler Fleetline of West Midlands PTE, an Alexander-bodied Leyland Atlantean of Merseyside PTE and a SELNEC Daimler Fleetline with Northern Counties body.

Far left: The London Dennis recovered by Mr Prince Marshall and restored is passed at the old Pimlico terminus of the 529 by a London Transport DMS-type Daimler Fleetline on the round-London tour.
S. W. Stevens-Stratten

Centre left: An East Kent AEC Regent V converted to open top on the seafront at Margate.
M&D and East Kent Bus Club

Left: Another open-top conversion for seaside service is this Leyland Titan of Eastbourne Borough Council. *C. Wilkin*

12
JOHNNIE WALKER
GJ 2098

294
Romford Gidea Park
Emerson Park
HORNCHURCH STATION
BUS STOP
LONDON TRANSPORT
EGN 409 J

Left: Preserved ex-Tilling AEC Regent ST971 at the Horse Guards Avenue terminus of vintage bus service 100 in 1972—behind it is an RT on 12, the route on which the ST spent much of its revenue-earning life. At the rear is an ex-Ribble/Standerwick Leyland Atlantean used on sightseeing tours by City Coach Lines. *V. H. Darling*

Below left: London Transport AEC Swift SMS409 in Emerson Park on service 294 in the spring of 1971. *J. Rickard*

Right: Before replacement of double-deckers on the Green Line services of London Country Bus Services, RCL2222 is seen approaching London Road garage, Romford (RE), on service 721. *J. Rickard*

Below: In the summer of 1970 London Transport SMS94 is seen at Edgware on the service thence to Harrow which was formerly a section of 18. *M. A. Penn*

17 Ventnor
XDL 799L
Tea Gardens

1 POOLE
1903
DAIMLER
HANTS & DORSET
VRU 126J
—by BUS
POOLE 34

Left: One of the Leyland National buses added to the Southern Vectis fleet in the summer of 1973 passes through Godshill one evening soon after delivery.
T. W. Moore

Below left: Ordered originally for Provincial, a Roe-bodied Daimler Fleetline of Hants & Dorset stands beside a Bristol KSW6B in Bournemouth bus station.
J. G. Carroll

Below: In 1971 City of Portsmouth Passenger Transport converted a 1956 Leyland Titan PD2 to open top; it is seen standing in front of one of the veteran Titan TD4s dating back to 1935 that was treated many years earlier.
David Rendell

15
CHICHESTER ROAD
EASTNEY
SOUTH PARADE PIER
DOCKYARD
OPNOR BRIDGE
188
PAY AS YOU ENTER
NO ENTRY
NO ENTRY
188
ATLANTEAN
RTP 188J

Left: Also in 1971, Portsmouth took delivery of a dozen Leyland Atlanteans with, somewhat unusually, single-deck bodies. They were built by Seddon. *David Rendell*

Above: Beginning its career with James of Ammanford and passing later to South Wales Transport, this Leyland Atlantean was by 1971 with City of Oxford and is loading in Gloucester Green bus station. It was destined to pass later to Derby Borough Transport. *T. W. Moore*

104
CIRCULAR TOUR
FEL 104L

Pevensey
Fisheries
4
BJK 680D
SUNLEY KINGS DRIVE
EASTBOURNE
SEE THE SHOW HOUSE
ITS A SHOW-PLACE
80
EASTBOURNE CORPORATION

Left: A Plaxton-bodied Leyland Leopard of Bournemouth Transport used for the undertaking's tours and for peak-hour services. *E. P. Sykes*

Below left: This Eastbourne Leyland Titan contrasts with the open-top conversion of a slightly newer bus illustrated on page 25. *W. T. Cansick*

Right: Single-deck underfloor-engined Guy Arabs were not all that common in municipal fleets but Southampton took delivery of four in 1954 with Park Royal bodywork, one of which is seen in Pound Tree Road in its later years.

Below: Another seaside single-decker is this Bristol RESL6G of Brighton, Hove & District with Eastern Coach Works body seen at Old Steine while still in red livery. *B. W. Spencer*

Left: An ex-London Transport RF in use by ABC Taxis (Blue Saloon), Guildford, on the local service which it started in 1973. *D. M. Stuttard*

Below: Bound for Birmingham in the summer of 1972, this Leyland Leopard of the Birmingham & Midland Motor Omnibus Co Ltd was the second of a batch of 49 with Duple Commander bodywork, many of which, including this one, were transferred to National Travel (South West) in 1976. *G. F. Walker*

Right: Somewhat out of the ordinary as an NBC fleet type is this Strachans-bodied Bedford VAM14 of Hants & Dorset photographed in Westover Road, Bournemouth. *B. W. Spencer*

Below right: Dual-purpose bodywork by Weymann is fitted to this AEC Reliance of Maidstone & District in National coach livery arriving at Victoria Coach Station from Maidstone. *G. F. Walker*

24
URNEMOUTH
JLJ 51E

LONDON
E1
Borough Green
West Malling
Rent a Ca
NATIONAL
2551
BKT 814C

Left: One of the surviving independent operators of bus services in Southern England is the Tillingbourne Bus Company which, in 1972, took delivery of a Willowbrook-bodied Bedford YRQ to bus grant specifications. It is seen in Peaslake on a short-lived Guildford-Horsham through service.
L. J. Barry

Centre left: A shortage of vehicles compelled London Country to hire double- and single-deckers from other operators in November 1975. Among them was this Weymann-bodied Daimler Fleetline of Bournemouth Transport seen here in Epsom High Street.
London Country

Below: After the taking over by Hants & Dorset of the operations of King Alfred, Winchester, the latter's Metro-Scania single-deckers were transferred to London Country Bus Services as an existing user of the type and allocated to Stevenage, where one of the three is seen wearing Superbus livery.
John Gowers

Above right: A Commer postbus stands while the driver delivers mail to houses between Coldharbour and Ockley on the service to and from Dorking. *L. J. Barry*

Centre right: For some years Thames Weald extended its Romford-Dartford-Sevenoaks service to Edenbridge, Horley, Gatwick Airport and Crawley and one of its Ford Transits stands at the bus station in the last-named in October 1971. *Edward Shirras*

Below: A successful independent operator of bus services within the London Transport area is Golden Miller of Feltham, which took delivery of this 49-seat Bristol LH with Plaxton Derwent bus body late in 1969.
S. W. Stevens-Stratten

Above: On loan to City of Oxford in the spring of 1971, a Daimler Fleetline of Maidstone & District loads in the Oxford bus station at Gloucester Green. *T. W. Moore*

Above right: Interchange between the National Bus Company and the Scottish Bus Group of Bristol Lodekkas and Bristol VRTs started in 1971 with 15 Eastern National FLFs swapped for a similar number of VRTs from Alexander (Midland). One of the latter leaves Basildon bus station in September of that year. *W. T. Cansick*

Right: Another NBC company which aided City of Oxford in its difficulties was Aldershot & District and an East Lancs-bodied Dennis Loline is here seen in 'The High' in March 1971. *T. W. Moore*

LONDON Kings Cross
SMS 45H

TO LET
INTERNATIONAL STORES
WEBBERS
WEBBERS
SECURICOR
radio
patrols
SAXTONROAD
360
SOU 468

AMFRICA LANE & BUS STN.
Western Road
Bentswood Road
84
SCD 501H

BASINGSTOKE
METRO-SCANIA
AOU 109J

M1
EXPRESS SERVICE
LONDON

Left: One of two Bristol VRTs which entered Southdown service at the end of June 1970 went first to Haywards Heath, where it is seen on the old-established town service. *M. P. M. Nimmo*

Below far left: This Metro-Scania of King Alfred, Winchester, provides a contrast with the view on page 36 of a similar vehicle with London Country.

Below left: One of the first of the 1965-66 batches of BMMO CM6T coaches for motorway service at Hyde Park Corner in National coach livery. *G. F. Walker*

Above: A 51-seat Willowbrook bus body on an AEC Reliance chassis added to the fleet of Safeguard Coaches, which has substantial urban bus operations at Guildford, in 1971. *Edward Shirras*

Below: One of the first of the London Country fleet to appear in new NBC livery was AEC Merlin MB91, seen here at Reigate. *London Country*

BURTON
tailoring
OLIVERS Shoes
43 Belgrave
138
METRO-SCANIA
WBC 138J

Left: When the single-deck Metro-Scania was announced in 1969 an early major operator to order was Leicester City Transport and the first batch began to arrive in March 1971. The third to be delivered is seen at work that summer. *T. W. Moore*

Above: A Leyland National of Nottingham City Transport at work on the central area service begun with Nationals hired from London Country but, by the autumn of 1973, maintained by the undertaking's own vehicles. *T. W. Moore*

Left: By 1976 Pilbeam's Harwich & Dovercourt Coaches fleet included one ex-Greater Manchester and one ex-Selnec Dennis Loline and a former Ribble Leyland Atlantean. *G. R. Mills*

Centre left: Another East Anglian independent, H. C. Chambers & Son of Bures, which started in 1916, took delivery of a Willowbrook-bodied Bedford YRQ, NCF 284M, in 1973. *G. R. Mortimer*

Bottom left: One of a pair of unusual Lex-Tillotson 45-seat school buses on Ford R1014 chassis of East Suffolk County Council is seen at East Bergholt Secondary School. *G. R. Mills*

Right: Duple Dominant Express bodies were fitted to a large batch of Bedford YRTs delivered to Barton Transport early in 1974.

Below: Similar bodywork was applied also to a YRT acquired by Theobald's Coaches of Long Melford in the previous year.

PRIVATE
Blue Bus Services

RAYLEIGH STATION
1
LEIGH HADLEIGH
THUNDERSLEY
SOUTHEND TRANSPORT
JTD 389P

Above left: Destruction by fire on the eve of Epiphany 1976 of virtually all the fleet of the Blue Bus Services operations of Derby Borough Transport makes particularly nostalgic this view of two of the Daimler Fleetlines in the old livery. That nearer the camera is the original Fleetline. *B. Goulding*

Above: One of 25 Bristol VRTs with Eastern Coach Works bodies delivered to Potteries Motor Traction in 1974 is seen in Longton with Aynsley's pottery kilns towering above it. *A. Moyes*

Left: Late in 1975 Southend Transport received six Daimler Fleetlines with Northern Counties bodies. They were registered in Bolton to obtain numbers coinciding with the fleet numbers. *G. R. Mills*

NOTTINGHAM ROAD
MANSFIELD CENTRE
CHESTERFIELD ROAD
PLEASLEY
102
912
MRB

Facing page: Standing at the Pleasley terminus of service 102 to Mansfield (Nottingham Road) is Mansfield District's Bristol Lodekka 597. *Terry Whitham*

Left: The close relationship of the Dennis Loline to the Lodekka is clear from this view, although this ex-Lancashire United vehicle has East Lancs bodywork. One of two bought by Canhams of Whittlesey, it is seen in March on the ex-Smith (Bluebell) service thence to Wisbech. *G. R. Mills*

Below: Normally used for training and for peak hour services, Southend Transport 316 Leyland Titan PD3 was brought out in May 1975 to work a shuttle service through floodwater at Hawkwell railway bridge. The normal Fleetlines turned each side of the water. *J. G. Lidstone*

Left: Rather unusually a United Counties Bristol RE with dual-purpose seating is seen in full National coach livery at Kettering bus station in the autumn of 1973. *G. J. Wadley*

Below: A Midland Red Leyland Leopard in poppy red and white dual-purpose livery, actually on local service in Rugby. *T. W. Moore*

Bottom: In red and cream, if somewhat dirty, ex-Midland General Bristol MW6G No 264 (262HNU) is seen in Buxton in January 1973 as Trent 166 on the ex-North Western service 85 to Glossop. *A. Moyes*

Right: Taken early in 1975, a Plaxton-bodied Ford R192 bought by R. W. Appleby Ltd with Hudsons Bus Co Ltd is in Bardney on the Horncastle-Lincoln service.
M. Fowler

Below: Willowbrook bodywork was mounted on a number of Bedford YRQs delivered to Barton Transport in 1971.
David R. Harman

Left: After long service with Nottingham City Transport three AEC Regent IIIs passed to Grimsby-Cleethorpes, where they were still hard at work in 1971, as evidenced by No 114. *A. Colley*

Below left: The Massey bodywork of this 1958 Leyland Titan PD3 of Southend Corporation Transport had been converted to open top by July 1971, when it was photographed in Leigh on Sea. *W. T. Cansick*

Right: Soon after entry into service in June 1971, one of a batch of lowheight Daimler Fleetlines of Southend Corporation Transport with Northern Counties bodies. *W. T. Cansick*

Below right: After delivery to Colchester Borough Transport in 1975 its ECW-bodied Leyland Atlanteans were modified by fitting quarterlights in the corner pillars. *M. A. Penn*

RAYLEIGH STATION
7
WJN 372J

1
AMBROSE AVENU
via Leather Bottl
60
COLCHESTER
LEYLAND
ATLANTEAN
JHK 500N

Right: An independent operator with a particularly high reputation for vehicle smartness is Delaine Coaches Ltd of Bourne and this Northern Counties-bodied Leyland Atlantean is no exception.
P. Sykes

Below: An early and uncommon version of the Bedford VAL was this one with Yeates Europa body and front and centre doors which started with Barton Transport as its No 965 and later passed to John Rannoch, a Stowmarket dairy supplier, for staff transport.
Roadrunner Productions

Right: One of two Leyland Titan PD2s originally with Wigan and subsequently with Greater Manchester PTE which were bought by East Staffordshire District Council in the summer of 1975. This one with Massey bodywork is seen in Burton-on-Trent. *T. W. Moore*

Below: New to Hudsons Bus Company of Horncastle, these two Leyland Titans passed to Holloways of Scunthorpe for its contract services. RFU 12 is a PD3 and OBE 964 a PD2. *M. Fowler*

VISIONHIRE
2
Stimpson Avenue
BUSHLAND ROAD
SAVE AT Argos Abington Square
GNH 597N

National Westminster Bank
116

Top left: In 1974 Northampton Transport brought in an extensive one-man-operation scheme. Among the vehicles which made it possible was No 33, one of a batch of Leyland Nationals, seen here in the town centre.
Michael Bennett

Left: Just repainted in NBC red, Marshall-bodied Bristol RE No 332 of Trent descends the main street in Bonsall, near Matlock. It was originally North Western 347.
A. Moyes

Top right: Apple pickers and graders of an Essex grower are given comfortable travel in an ex-Grey Green Coaches Leyland Leopard with Duple Northern 41-seat body.
G. R. Mills

Above: An unusual addition to the Eastern National fleet in the spring of 1971 was a Leyland Tiger Cub with Metro-Cammell bodywork which had previously been R368 in the East Midland fleet. It and a similar vehicle were the first Tiger Cubs in the ENOC fleet and the first Leyland single-deckers for many years. *J. G. Lidstone*

Right: The first of a batch of five AEC Swifts with East Lancs bodywork delivered to Ipswich Corporation Transport in 1973. *G. R. Mills*

Right: New to Bournemouth Corporation in 1954, this Burlingham-bodied Leyland Royal Tiger is seen about 19 years later as Burton-on-Trent No 2 in that undertaking's new red, white and green livery. *G. R. Mills*

Below: In the summer of 1973 a SELNEC (Southern) Bristol RELL with Alexander bodywork ex-North Western passes an elderly Trent dual-purpose Leyland Tiger Cub on the former North Western service from its new depot at Buxton. *A. Moyes*

17 KINGS HEATH
UNH 9L

GB HUDSONS GB
HUDSONS TOURS
LINCOLN
BARDNEY
HORNCASTLE
NBE 463M
8A

Left: When Northampton decided to adopt single-deck operation on a substantial scale 20 Daimler Fleetlines with Willowbrook bodies were ordered and came into service in the earlier part of 1973. As indicated on page 57 a dozen Leyland Nationals followed in 1974. *M. Fowler*

Below left: A connection in the Lincolnshire village of Horsington by the ex-Hudsons Bus Horncastle-Lincoln service of Appleby with the Horsington-Woodhall Spa-Boston route (8A) of Lincolnshire Road Car. *M. Fowler*

Above right: A Leyland Leopard with Weymann bodywork originally in the Sheffield Transport Department fleet waits at the Middleton terminus of the service to Chesterfield operated by Hulley of Baslow. *M. Fowler*

Right: Another Derbyshire independent, Woolliscroft of Darley Dale, had by 1972 obtained this Roe-bodied AEC Reliance originally Doncaster Corporation 29 and later Golden Miller, Feltham. *M. Fowler*

Below: With Willowbrook 008 bodywork a Bedford YMT of National Travel (South East) leaves Doncaster Southern bus station on service 352 for Colchester via Peterborough and Cambridge. *M. Fowler*

WALSALL
32
FOOTWEAR
ces
BGY 424H
VOH 23J

Left: A Daimler Fleetline of West Midlands PTE in Stafford Street, Walsall, before dismantling of the wires for the then recently abandoned trolleybus system.
T. W. Moore

Above: Still in service in February 1974 was Chester City Transport's oldest vehicle, a Massey-bodied Guy Arab (No 1). *A. Moyes*

Left: Crosville Bristol RELL6G No SRG15 crosses the Clettwr River bridge at Tre'rddol on its way back to its home depot at Machynlleth from Aberystwyth. *A. Moyes*

Below: An ex-Edinburgh Leyland Titan PD2 bought in 1970 by Cream Line of Tonmawr together with another to replace ex-Southdown Titans on contract work and the service between Neath and Tonmawr. *G. H. Truran*

Right: Originally Neath & Cardiff and sold by Western Welsh in May 1974, this Duple-bodied AEC Reliance became No 10 in the fleet of Byrnes of Leek, the Berresford associate. *G. H. Truran*

Below right: Carrying a fleet number in a style somewhat outdated in comparison with the modern appearance of the Metro-Scania is No 13 in what was then the Pontypridd UDC fleet. *A. Moyes*

PRIVATE
10
10
BYRNES of Leek
CTX 986C
Pedigree

TREFOREST VIA QUEEN ST.
13
METRO-SCANIA
NTX 325L

FISHGUARD

Left: A 1956 Leyland Tiger Cub of Western Welsh (1139: MUH 139) skirts the coast near Trevine on January 9 1971, the last day of operation of the St Davids-Fishguard service. *A. Moyes*

Above: One of five Leyland Leopards with Duple Dominant bodies delivered to the North Western company, at that time (1973) a Ribble subsidiary, climbing into Aberystwyth on the X4 service from Manchester. *A. Moyes*

Below: An early morning departure for a Scottish tour is made from Coventry in September 1975 by a 12-metre Leyland Leopard of Wallace Arnold with a 57-seat Plaxton body and an 11.1-litre Leyland engine. *T. W. Moore*

Right: Devon General 46, a 1968 AEC Reliance with Willowbrook body, appeared in a new livery at Exeter in the summer of 1971. *Edward Shirras*

Centre right: A dual-purpose Seddon Pennine of Princess Bus Service (Duggins) in Ironmarket, Newcastle-under-Lyme, on the service thence to Silverdale. *A. Moyes*

Bottom right: The nature of the Birmingham Centrebus service provided by the West Midlands PTE has changed a good deal since one of the Commer minibuses was painted in a conspicuous orange livery in the summer of 1973. *T. W. Moore*

1

NEWTON ABBOT
TORQUAY
EXPRESS SERVICE
46
DEVON GENERAL
DEVON GENERAL
LUO 46F

SILVERDALE
SEDDON
TRE 675L

Dixons
CENTREBUS
EOF 241L
LET

372
GLOUCESTER
LIMITED STOP
6445
Midland Red
CHA 445K

470
SWINDON
622
XLJ 727K

Left: A dual-purpose 49-seat Willowbrook bodywork is fitted to this Midland Red Leyland Leopard seen in Gloucester bus station in February 1972. *Michael Bennett*

Below left: Another dual-purpose body, this time by Eastern Coach Works, on a Wilts & Dorset Bristol RELL which is entering Swindon bus station in February 1972 on the service from Salisbury worked jointly with Bristol Omnibus. *Michael Bennett*

Above right: Seen in January 1974 resplendent in West Midlands PTE colours is BMMO-built S22 which kept its old fleet number 5902 when transferred from Midland Red with the Birmingham area routes in the previous month. *B. L. Thompson*

Centre right: A Willowbrook-bodied Bedford of Grenville, Camborne, at Falmouth Moor in 1973 on the Penryn service then shared with the Penryn & Falmouth company shortly to be taken over by Grenville. *T. H. J. Dethridge*

Below: South Wales Plaxton-bodied AEC Reliance 461 was the last vehicle to be delivered to Neath & Cardiff Luxury Coaches during its separate existence; by November 1973 it had come to local duties in Llanelli. *A. Moyes*

Above: Midland Red Daimler Fleetline 5273 on hire to City of Oxford and repainted as its 909 but retaining BMMO legal lettering. *S. Jolly*

Below: A convertible open-top Bristol Lodekka transferred from Crosville to Bristol Omnibus in 1973 is seen in Weston-super-Mare the following year. *M. A. Penn*

Above centre: A Park Royal-bodied Daimler CVG6 of the Swindon undertaking before its renaming as Thamesdown in 1974.

Above right: Early in 1974 Plymouth City Transport withdrew its last rear-platform Leyland Titan PD2s from service and the occasion was marked by a special tour organised by the Plymouth Bus Club. *Plymouth Bus Club*

Below: Shortly before its business was taken over by Midland Red in 1973 Green Bus Company of Rugeley made the last addition to its fleet with this ex-Cumberland Bristol Lodekka. It forms a comparison with the open-top version of the earlier model shown opposite. *M. Fowler*

Above: Plymouth has long been an inveterate Leyland user and few other makes have been bought in any quantity. No 75 was the first of a batch of 15 delivered in 1975 with Park Royal bodywork on Atlantean chassis. *J. P. Stothard*

Above right: Originally with Kippax & District, this Leyland Titan PD3A with Roe bodywork had migrated by early 1972 to the rather variegated fleet of Stonier, Goldenhill. *A. Moyes*

Lower right: The first Bristol to enter the fleet of Hutchings & Cornelius, South Petherton, was this ECW-bodied LH6L seen at Taunton on the service to South Petherton. *D. Withers*

STONIERS
10
556 DUA

H&O
TAUNTON
GYC 160K

Left: An all-too-familiar feature of the 1970s exemplified by a notice outside the Pembrokeshire depot of Western Welsh in St Davids. *A. Moyes*

Below: During the reconstruction of the Britannia railway bridge across the Menai Strait after the bad fire, train passengers were carried in special Crosville buses between Bangor station and the reopened halt at Llanfair PG. Bristol Lodekka DLG946 is seen at the latter during the summer of 1971. *J. H. Price*

Right: While Garner Street was closed in 1971 alternate journeys on the Potteries service 37 between Newcastle-under-Lyme and Hanley used Etruscan Street, Stoke-on-Trent, and PMT H6650, one of the then surviving Daimler CVG5s with lightweight Metro-Cammell bodies, passes through the Stoke gasworks. *A. Moyes*

HANLEY
37
XVT 650
NO PARKING

73
GLOUCESTER
CARDIFF
175

ASSOCIATED MOTORWAYS
CHELTENHAM SPA
4876 DF

Left: The driver of a Red & White Bristol RE finds it not quite possible to squeeze between two similar vehicles at Cardiff bus station.
L. F. Watson

Below left: Early in 1971 two Black & White Leyland Leopards at Gloucester Green bus station, Oxford, display a livery change with 236 in the foreground wearing the old and 230 in the background in the then new NBC style.
M. D. Shaw

Above right: One of five Plaxton-bodied Bristol RE coaches which entered service with the Grey Cars subsidiary of Greenslades in the summer of 1971.
G. H. Truran

Centre right: Plaxton bodywork was fitted also to two Leyland Leopards which went to work the following year for Llynfi Motor Services of Maesteg. *G. H. Truran*

Below: A Bedford YRQ chassis forms the basis of this Plaxton Elite Express body for Parish, of Morda, near Oswestry. *J. G. Carroll*

Left: Waiting to leave Barnstaple for Westward Ho! in 1971 is a recently delivered Bristol RE of Western National. *Edward Shirras*

Below: A contrast to the coaches illustrated on the previous page is provided by the ex-South Wales AEC Regent V of Llynfi Motor Services. *G. H. Truran*